MYSTERY MOTORS

Honest John's
MYSTERY MOTORS

CONSTABLE

LONDON

First published in the UK in 2001 by Constable,
an imprint of Constable & Robinson Ltd
Reprinted 2002

Constable & Robinson Ltd
3 The Lanchesters
162 Fulham Palace Road
London W6 9ER
www.constablerobinson.com

A copy of the British Library Cataloguing in
Publication Data is available from the British Library.

ISBN 1-84119-430-1

The images in this book are taken from Honest John's Mystery Motors website, www.mysterymotors.com.
While efforts have been made to contact the owner of each picture used for the purpose of this book, in some
cases this has not proved possible. The publishers would like to take the opportunity to thank anyone who has
not been contacted, and invite them to write with proof of ownership so that a complimentary copy of the book
may be sent.

CONTENTS

PREFACE

Mystery Motors began as an offshoot of my Motoring Agony Column in *The Daily Telegraph* Motoring section every Saturday.

The trouble was, readers sent in so many pictures of old cars for identification that they began to swamp the Agony column. The only way we could cope with them was to start a separate Mystery Motors column.

But the paper couldn't always guarantee to find space for it. Up to eight Mystery Motors columns could be backed up in the editor's in-tray while anxious readers waited month after month for return of their precious photographs. Then it got worse. As part of the re-formatting of the *Telegraph* Motoring, the Honest John column was re-jigged to run just a single 'Mystery Motor' each Saturday, giving even less possibility of publication. All I could do in the circumstances was find some other way of publishing and preserving the pictures. And so, in Spring 2000, *www.mysterymotors.com* was born.

This meant that if I was in doubt about an identity I could scan it into my computer, run it on the website and ask the whole world for help. But, of course, not everyone is on the Internet. Particularly those amongst us most likely to appreciate photographs taken during the first three decades of the last century.

That's why we've compiled the pictures from the Mystery Motors website into an album.

If you have a Mystery Motor you would like identifying, please either e-mail a compressed JPEG (ideally 4 inches across; at 300dpi; no more than 5 inches across and no more than 400dpi) to *letters@honestjohn.co.uk* Or send the photo with a SAE for its return to: Mystery Motors, Motoring Desk, The Daily Telegraph, 1 Canada Square, Canary Wharf, London E14 5DT.

Honest John

INTRODUCTION

Years ago, a reader wrote: "While rummaging through some old photographs, my wife turned up a picture of her great uncle, on the back of which is inscribed, 'Charlie SANTLER – builder of the 1st car in England.' He lived in Malvern, Worcestershire and, at the time of the picture, taken around 1920, he was more then sixty years old. So, assuming he was about thirty when he built the car, he must have done so between 1880 and 1890. It would be most interesting to know if any of your readers can shed more light on this."

I ran the picture and, amazingly, the current owner of the car replied.

Registered "AB 171:, the Santler car survives in full running order in Monmouth and regularly takes part in the annual Emancipation Run from London to Brighton. To appreciate the full story of Charlie Santler's sterling efforts a bit of history is required.

In 1863 Jean-Joseph Etienne Lenoir drove the World's first internal combustion engined car from Paris to Joinville-le-Pont. In the UK, though, backward thinking held back the birth of the motor industry. The Red Flag Act of 1865 decreed words to the effect that at least three persons shall be employed to drive or conduct such a locomotive – one to precede it on foot carrying a red flag constantly displayed – and that any person with a horse and carriage could stop it simply by raising their hand.

The Act also imposed a speed limit of 4 mph in the country and 2 mph in towns, while the Highways and Locomotive (Amendment) Act of 1878 laid down the first emissions regulations by requiring that a mechanical vehicle "should consume its own smoke".

This ludicrous legislation left the field open for Panhard et Levassor, Gottlieb Daimler and Karl Benz to build the first practical cars elsewhere. Charles Santler worked with Benz on the very early three-wheeler cars. But he fell out with the great man, possibly over his own ideas for creating a steerable four-wheeler car, returned to Malvern Link and, in 1889, with the aid of his brother Walter, began to build "The first four wheeler car in Britain". (The similar Benz 'Velo' was not launched until 1894.)

Santler's 'Malvernia' was first powered by a steam engine, later replaced by a gas engine in 1892 and finally a petrol engine in 1894. It was laid up in a blacksmith's yard from the late 1890s until around 1907 and then appears to have been parked near a cricket pavilion, where it deteriorated quite badly.

Research reveals that other cars were built from scratch by Frederick Bremer of Walthamstowe between 1892 and 1894 (this car survives, registration "NJ 733"); Herbert Austin, who built the first Wolseley tri-car in 1895 (this also survives at the Heritage Centre, Gaydon); and Frederick Lanchester who built his first, totally original, car in 1895. One book credits an alternative builder of the first truly 'British' motor car as Edward Butler, at the Merryweather Fire Engine Works in Greenwich in 1888.

Yet another scratch-built creation was a tri-car constructed by Albert Farnell in 1897. The specification was: independent 'sliding pillar' front suspension, 1.25hp air cooled motor, tubular chassis, belt drive via three step cone pulleys (an early CVT). Farnell later fitted a Starley rear axle, his own patent 4-speed non-crash gearbox and worm and sector steering by wheel rather than lever.

Beyond these six, my sources tell me that other cars built in the UK before 1900 were close imitations of Panhards (Coventry Daimlers and MMCs) or Benz Velos (Marshalls from Manchester, Stars from Wolverhampton and Arnolds from Paddock Wood in Kent).

Charles Santler went on to build light front-engined cars in 1906 and 1913, then diversified into manufacturing a motor plough in the 1920s. His possible claim to fame as the 'builder of the 1st car in

INTRODUCTION

England' stayed unremarked for years, until the reader sent me her modest-quality print of the Santler parked outside a cricket pavilion.

Since then, literally hundreds of pictures have come and gone. I've often got the identifications wrong and have been corrected by acknowledged expert Mike Worthington-Williams, so I am delighted he agreed to help with this book. I'd also like to thank Nick Baldwin, Nick Georgano, David Burgess Wise, Henk Schurring and the many others who have identified cars or put right my attempts from the newspaper columns and the website.

The main thing about these pictures is that if they weren't published in the column, on the website and in this book, they might remain forgotten in some dark recess of an old desk or fusty photograph album in someone's attic. Instead, here they are, reviving memories, stirring up nostalgia and most important of all giving pleasure to everyone turning these pages.

Long may they do so, and the more old pictures you continue to send in, the bigger and better we can make the next Mystery Motors album.

THE ARCHIVE

This beautiful looking alloy bodied car (left) appears to be a 1926 two litre six-cylinder AC.
An AC Light Six was the first British car to win the Monte Carlo Rally, in 1926, driven by
Victor Bruce and W. J. Parnell.

Michael Chandler of Shillington sent this photo (right) showing a car of his grandfather, Robert Asketer.
It's an AC Sociable 5/6hp built from 1908 to 1914. This looks like one of the earlier cars.

AJS

Tony Scarth of Woodbridge sent us this photo of an AJS he bought for his wife in 1955. The AJS 9hp was a conventional little car built between 1930 and 1933. It had a long stroke 1,018cc Coventry Climax side-valve four cylinder engine developing 24bhp at 3,000rpm and a four speed gearbox. Bodies were either two seater roadsters, fabric saloons or coachbuilt saloons. Around 3,300 were made, but the company went bust in 1931 and was sold to Willys-Crossley who kept production going until 1933.

ALLDAYS

This picture, sent by Robert Asketer, is believed to be a 1914 Alldays Midget 1,100cc which grew out of the earlier 990cc Midget, some of which had this distinctive bullnose radiator.

ANGUS-SANDERSON

Identified as a 1921 Angus-Sanderson 14.3hp, reg "R 5135". Mike Worthington-Williams says it was originally supplied new by A.R. Atkey & Sons of Derby to a Mr Bradley and remained in "Bradleys Barn" for many years after he stopped using it. It was later restored by John Foy of Royston, Herts at the same time as Worthy was working on his own Angus-Sanderson. During the concurrent restorations, numerous parts were copied which greatly helped the process. It was sold by Christie's to David Howard of Romsey who re-sold it to a member of the Sanderson family who now resides in France.

ARGYLL

Michel Boyd of Aylesbury asked about this car owned by his grandfather in 1904. The vertical tube radiator means that it is almost certainly an Argyll 5hp of around 1903 (earlier models had tiller steering).

ARROL-JOHNSTON

This was identified as a 1911 Arrol-Johnston 15.9hp, bearing the same "CK 644" registration as the owner's previous Rover.

ASTON MARTIN

This 1937 Aston Martin Speed model was successfully traced. The photo was sent by David Funk of Halifax and had been taken soon after the car's restoration by ex-David Brown engineer Bill Smith of Oakenshaw in 1985. Thirteen Claud Hill-designed 'Speed' chassis were built, initially for the cancelled 1936 Le Mans 24 hour race. This car was originally built with an ugly single seater body and a special Cross rotary valve cross-flow engine was developed for it but never fitted, for an unsuccessful attempt on the 2.0 litre

Outer Circuit record at Brooklands. After the war it was purchased by Gordon Gartside of Knaresborough in 1947 who fitted the attractive one-off two seater body and registered the car for road use "KWX 638". Its last racing appearance was at Silverstone in 1951 after which it was laid up until Bill Smith found it fitted with a 4-cylinder DB1 engine. He rebuilt it for a Mr Uberg. Later, Andy Bell of pre-war Aston Martin Specialists Ecurie Bertelli of Otley acquired the car from Mr Uberg, sold the body to a Japanese collector, installed a genuine 1930's "Speed" engine and is in the process of rebuilding the car as a single seater to its 1939 specification.

AN APPARITION

And presently, while we still waited in the coolness of that early May morning listening to the birds that now began to sing more heartily, there fell on our ears another signal, this time of ominous portent. Far away among the fields of the lower valleys, like the firing of heavy guns, resounded the first of a series of echoing detonations . . . It must have been three miles away when we heard it first, for several minutes passed before the explosions, instantly increasing in volume, became so deafening as to assure us of the immediate arrival of the machine. Then it appeared, growing like the insect of a nightmare, enormously bigger and louder; slowed down and drew up beside us; and, for once obedient to the will of its driver, roared itself out into quietness. Then we were able to speak to the man and hear the tale of his journey. It was wild enough. He was covered, even to his face, with oil which was flying up out of some neglected orifice; his frail seat had given way beneath him and he was shaken and bounced precariously over the fatal chains and wheels of his charge; the covering of a metal switch controlling the passage of electric fluid to the vitals of the engine had come off; so that even to modify the speed of the insane projectile upon which he rode he must instantly keep pressing the thumb upon the sharp and lacerating point of the switch, receiving an electric shock as well as a flesh wound every time. "It isn't as if I had nothing else to do," he remarked with singular moderation, as he wiped the oil and sweat from his face and the blood from his fingers; "but at any rate she goes!" And he turned again cheerfully to his really appalling task. The engine was restarted in a clap of thunder, and with a six-foot flash of yellow flame the car rushed away, booming like a minute-gun long after it was out of sight.

(from The Complete Motorist, *by A. B. Filson Young, 1904)*

AUSTRO-DAIMLER

Identified by David Burgess-Wise as a circa 1913 Austro-Daimler
probably updated to look post WW1.

P. Pumfrey sent this photo of what he thought was an A.V. Monocar of circa 1920 and asked for information about it. The Monocar was built by Ward and Avey Ltd at Teddington, Middlesex. According to historian Nick Baldwin (*A–Z of Cars of the 1920s*) the factory employed eighty men and several hundred cars were produced between 1919 and 1924. The car in the photo would have had a 5hp to 8hp JAP, Blackburn or Swiss MAG engine in the tail, a foot-operated two-speed epicyclic gearbox or a Sturmey Archer three speeder and chain drive.

BEAN

Rex Tester contacted me to ask what the Bean car in which his father passed his driving test in 1928 might have looked like. Thanks to D.W. of Westbury-on-Severn I have this print of a Bean 11.9hp, built from 1919 to 1927. It was purchased second-hand by his father for £400 in 1921 and re-sold for £160 in 1923.

BEAN

This was identified by Mike Worthington-Williams as an export model Bean Imperial Six of 1927. It has been repatriated from Australia by another reader who is in the process of restoring it.

BEDELIA

Philip Radford of Southend-on-Sea sent us this postcard print of a publicity vehicle once thought to have belonged to a family member who lived in Southminster, Essex and had a business on the High Street. Gerry Killey of South Woodham Ferrers identified it as a 4hp Bedelia cycle car built in France. It was belt-driven with a single cylinder engine of 82mm bore. The registration was "F 9638" and was issued to Henry Leonard Buxton of Southminster on 12 November 1914.

BELSIZE

I first got the identity of the car on the right of this old postcard print wrong. It is actually a Belsize 10/12hp of around 1913 and not a Humber as I had thought. Many thanks to Brian Demaus of The Humber Register for the correction. The two other vehicles are Model T Fords converted by Baico into a bus and a charabanc. The conversion involved stretching the chassis and taking the drive by chains from the original Ford axle (shackled solidly to the chassis) to a second rear axle some two feet aft.

BENTLEY

A bit of fun here. D. M. of Littleover sent these two photos of a car snapped at Olympia in 1960. I immediately thought it must have been a film car, but *The Great Race* was set in 1908 and *Those Magnificent Men in their Flying Machines* at about the same time, and both films were shot in 1960. The title. *Monte Carlo or Bust* sprung to mind, but I couldn't find it in any of my directories. David Burgess-Wise came to the rescue with the information that the car was built for the film *School for Scoundrels* in which a pair of dodgy salesmen played by Peter Jones and Dennis Price sell the car to Ian Carmichael who hopes he can use it to impress Janette Scott. The cad of the picture was played by Terry-Thomas who drove a disguised Aston Martin DB3.

The exact off-screen identity of the car pictured on page 29 remained a mystery until Peter Heywood of Marlborough found it in Johnnie Green's *Bentley 50 Years of the Marque*. It was built on the chassis of a 4.5 litre Bentley. The current owner, Neil Twyman, then sent in the picture above and the information that it is a 1928 4.5 litre, chassis number AB 3363. His father purchased it as the Swiftmobile from Associated British Picture Corporation at Elstree in 1961 and commenced restoration back to a Bentley. This was finished in the early 1970s and the car went on to win the 1974 BDC Concours at Kensington Gardens.

Easily identified as a Benz Velo of the mid 1890s. Many late nineteenth century cars were copies of the Benz.

BLERIOT-WHIPPET

John Hissey sent this photo of his father in one of his later cars which John thinks replaced an unreliable Calcott. David Burgess-Wise quickly identified it as a Bleriot-Whippet, built in Addlestone, near Weybridge, during 1920–27.

BRISTOL

This bus was thought by Noel Thomas of St Austell to be possibly run by Great Western Railways on the Perranporth–St Agnes–Porthowan-Redruth route. However, Mike Wademan states that GWR never operated the route. He thinks that the operator was most likely Cornwall Motor Transport which started a Perranporth–St Agnes–Porthowan–Redruth service in 1924. If this is correct, then the bus was a Bristol 4-ton chassis fitted with a 30-seat Bristol body.

Identified as two examples of 1938 BSAs, both 9hp front-wheel-drive Scout models.

BUCKINGHAM

John Netherwood of Stocksmore sent this photo of a cyclecar said to have been given by his grandfather to his mother when she was fourteen, in which case the date would have been prior to WWI. It had individual belt drives to each of the rear wheels, but had me stumped. Tim Harding identified it as a pre-WW1 Buckingham, which was quite a sporty cyclecar.

The photograph on the left was identified by Henk Schuuring as a Buick B55 of 1915/1916 and not a Cadillac as I had previously thought.

The photograph on the right which was sent in is a circa 1926 Buick Six.

DAIMLER

A lady from Haltwhistle in Northumberland sent this picture of her mother-in -law riding in the car owned by her godfather, Sir George Sutton, registered "D312". David Burgess-Wise identified it as a 22hp Coventry Daimler, circa 1903.

DARRACQ

Dick Sheppard sent this photo, dated circa 1924, of "CH 924" with passengers "suitably dressed for an East Coast Holiday". He rightly guessed it to be of French origin, as it is either a Cottin-Desgouttes or a 16hp Darracq of pre-WW1 design built 1913–19.

DELAHAYE

Ian Cameron identified this car, previously thought to be a Chrysler Six, as
a French Delahaye, most likely to be a six-cylinder Type 112 "coach"
of the late 1920s.

DE DION BOUTON

This shows a 1904 8hp de Dion Bouton, one of the most popular cars of the day, characterized by its bonnet style and by its advanced de Dion semi-independent rear axle. Darracqs of the same period look similar from the front but have different spring dumb-irons.

SEATING ARRANGEMENTS

I shall never forget my own first drive in a car. It was in July, 1901. A friend who had just purchased a de Dion car wished to show it off to me. In the course of a short drive in the West End we were stopped by a traffic block going up the Haymarket. I was seated on his left and talking to him, when he was suddenly obliterated from my sight by a horse's head and neck which was thrust between us; a hansom cab behind us had been obliged to pull up with a jerk, as we had been; the slobbering, frothing mouth, well in front of us, spread equine spray all over our faces, while the unhappy horse champed with restlessness and apprehension at an evil-smelling, amazing looking vehicle such as he had never seen before.

The reader has only to look at the photograph to see how the horse could not do otherwise than thrust his head and neck unexpectedly between us, and interrupt our conversation. There was nothing behind our seat: it was as if we were driving about in a double armchair, or settee, drawn by a horse.

But this experience did not deter me. I was so thrilled by my short drive that I went straight off to de Dion's agent, and in return for a cheque for three hundred guineas became the proud possessor of a then quite new, latest model 4½ h.p. de Dion-Bouton Voiturette …I tried my hand at driving and steering in the quiet country lanes of Herefordshire …Self-starters were unknown in those days. On many occasions was I the cause of holding up all the traffic, with my car broadside across the road, while I ground wearily and hopefully with the starting handle, cursing and sweating the while, my hat falling off, and my glasses becoming steamed.

(from The Dawn of Motoring, *by Kenneth Murchison, 1942)*

An F. Hearn of Walsall bodied ambulance thought to be on an American Dodge Bros or Graham Bros chassis. (The same chassis were sold under the two different names.) The flat top bonnet would date it as 1920–28, probably towards the end of this period on account of the drum headlights and larger section tyres. Many thanks to Nigel Skellern of Walsall for the photo.

FIAT

Bill Cole asked about this 1930s sports car, which is an example of the charming 995cc FIAT 508S Balilla 2-seater of which around 1,200 were built between 1934 and 1937.

FLANDERS

Robert McCowatt asked about the Flanders car in a family photograph taken in 1922. The Flanders 20 was a light car built by Everitt-Metzger-Flanders Co. of Detroit, Michigan from 1909 to 1912 and marketed by Studebaker. It had a four cylinder 2.5 litre engine. Early 1909 models had a two-speed transmission, but this was soon replaced by a three-speeder. (Information from *The Beaulieu Encyclopedia of the Automobile.*)

Chris Rueb of Benissa in Alicante sent this photo of his mother on her honeymoon in Indonesia and asked the make of the car. It looks like a Ford Model A Roadster, built from 1928 to 1931. Indonesia must have been amazing in those days.

FORD

Paul Hambling of the Museum of Dartmoor Life asked me to identify the cars in this photo outside the garages of Day & Sons in Okehampton. These are all Model T Fords circa 1920.

Nick Webster sent a photograph of his great uncle (Alfred Nelson Greenwood) at the wheel of his newly made open tourer, thought to be circa 1910. He understands that he had the coachbuilding done at a garage in Lancaster and the other two men in the car could be the chaps who did the work. He asked the make of the chassis, which is a post-WW1 Model T Ford, possibly of 1920 vintage but definitely not 1910.

FRANKLIN

Identified by Worthington-Williams as an air-cooled American Franklin around 1917–1919. The Renault-type bonnet was adopted in 1911 and continued until the "horse collar" grille of 1921.

FULLER

Spotted in Australia, this is a rare 1910 Fuller buggy, built by the Fuller Buggy Co. of Jackson, Michigan just from 1909 to 1910. The company also made "high wheelers", with horse-drawn wagon type wheels, which had chain drive. The model shown had shaft drive, four cylinder engine and full-elliptical springs.

GALLOWAY

Identified as a 1923 Galloway 10/20. Production was begun in 1921 by Dorothee Pullinger in a WW1 aero engine factory at Tongland, Kirkcudbright using a largely female workforce. The car was based on the Fiat 501, had a side-valve four cylinder 1,460cc engine, three, then later four speed gearbox and was slow but reliable. In 1922 production switched to the Arrol-Johnston factory at Heathall. Two 10/20s were among the five cars that finished the 1922 RSAC 6 days trial without any problems.

HILLMAN

Recognizable as a 1935 Hillman Minx 6-light saloon, which had a 1,185cc side-valve four cylinder engine. It differed from the 1934 model in having an unbroken row of bonnet louvres; it also had synchromesh on 1st gear.

HORCH

Identified as a 1937–43 Horch Type 108. It had a 3,823cc Horch V8 engine, selectable four wheel drive, short front and rear overhangs and twin side mounted spare wheels mounted on an axle to give underbody protection when cresting hills.

HUMBER

Aiden Liddell's Humber was positively identified by John Tarring of The Humber Register as a 3,479cc 1908 15hp Coventry Humber. The car, complete with Cape Cart Hood and Windscreen, would have cost £338-8s-0d when new. The Stepney spare rim was an extra £3-18s-0d, plus £7-5s-6d for a tyre and tube. 1908 was the year Humber closed its works at Beeston, Nottingham and moved all production to its second factory in Coventry.

HUMBER

Paul Hambling of the Museum of Dartmoor Life asked me to identify the car in this photo outside the garages of Day & Sons in Okehampton. "T 1079" is a Beeston Humber, circa 1906.

After much research, Henk Schuuring from Holland whittled down the photograph on the left to either a Swift or a Humber, both circa 1908. I'm pretty sure it is a late Beeston Humber, circa 1908.

R. Dryden of Great Bookham asked about this car photographed in the 1950s with its owner, Keith Harrison. It is a Humber Snipe Utility, based on the 1939 Snipe limousine chassis, with an 85bhp six cylinder side valve engine. This example is still on its desert tyres so could have seen service in North Africa.

JOWETT

David Watson of Wrexham asked about this car owned by his grandfather in Kenya in 1924. It is a Jowett 7hp short-two, circa 1923, which had a 907cc engine and benefited from the RAC formula for taxing horsepower by having only two cylinders. There are eight pictures of identical cars in Noel Stokoe's *Images of Motoring: Jowett 1901–1954.*

Peter Mason sent me a photo of another Jowett, this a circa 1925 7hp long-four containing his great aunt and mother in the back seat. His mother still remembers the Jowett with affection. The photo was taken in Waterloo, Liverpool in the late 1920s. In 1926 the Metropolitan Police took delivery of twenty-seven Jowett long-fours.

KARRIER

Sent in by John Richards of Kingswinford, this is a Karrier Type WDS (War Department Subsidy) of which 2,200 were built between 1914 and 1921, initially for WWI of 1914-1918. Those that were repatriated were fitted with civilian lorry, charabanc or even open-topped double-decker bus bodies. Charabancs were very popular for outings from around 1912 to around 1925 after which they were gradually replaced by "all weather" coaches.

Il Re e la Regina d'Italia in automobile

4761.

Henk Schuuring from Holland identified this car being driven by Victor Emmanuel, King of Italy. It is a petrol-electric Krieger (a German name; French marque). Both front wheels were driven by electric hub motors. The car was made under licence in Italy from 1905 to 1913, but after 1907 the company was re-named STAE Societa Torinese Automobili.

LATIL

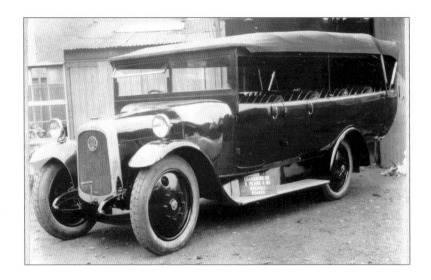

This Latil charabanc was bodied by coachbuilders F. Hearn & Co of Walsall. It is thought to be a Type B chassis dating from the early 1920s. Latils were French vehicles built at Suresnes from 1898 to 1956. George Latil was famous for adapting the de Dion axle for front wheel drive and from 1914 built the Latil LL, a four wheel drive, four wheel steered road tractor. The four cylinder Type B was very popular in the 1920s and 1930s. Many thanks to Nigel Skellern of Walsall for the photo.

LOZIER

E. S. of Andover sent this photo of her grandmother, who travelled extensively over Europe, Africa and the USA, taken in April 1912. David Burgess-Wise identified the car as a circa 1911 Lozier Type 51 Lakewood Torpedo built in Toledo, Ohio, with a 9-litre six cylinder engine.

MERCEDES

The photo of this very early Mercedes 40hp (left), probably 1902, was sent by J. Morris of Leighton Buzzard. The driver of the car was Robert Watson who held a French driving licence dating from 1907 (actually a photocard bearing his picture). At the time he was chauffeur to a Miss Barbour who married a Mr Andrews, the designer of the *Titanic* who drowned when the ship went down. She then married Mr Harland of Harland and Wolff, who built the *Titanic*.

Colonel Forbes sent this photo of "LB 3741" (right) taken after 1911 and which I thought was either a Mercedes or a Benz. David Burgess-Wise confirmed that the car was one of Gordon Watney's ·stable of racing Mercedes which were kept at Cobham.

T. S. of Lytham asked about this car, Leeds registered "U 133", which, from the radiator and chain-drive cog wheels, I think is a Mercedes 40/60 of 1904–06. A. V. Parker DFC found in a booklet entitled "Old Lakeland Transport" that Kaiser Wilhelm gave a Mercedes to Lord Lonsdale and that the delivery driver, Johann Kieser, agreed to become Lonsdale's chauffeur. He speculates that the location was therefore Lowther Castle, Lord Lonsdale's home.

MINERVA

Roger Kirkpatrick of Broadstairs asked for confirmation that the car in the photo was a Minerva. He bought a Minerva for £30 in 1951 where it formed part of a chicken run. The car started straight away and he was able to drive it out of the field. But it leaked and ruined his young lady's new hat, forcing him to feel obliged to propose to her, hence the car's importance in his family history. I'm pretty sure it is a Minerva AB 12CV, built from 1927 to 1933, with a 2.0 litre 6-cylinder engine famous for its appetite for oil.

THE GENTLE ART OF STARTING

Having satisfied yourself that the car is in perfect running order, the next procedure is to turn on the cock under the petrol tank, take the connecting plug from your pocket and put it into position, take the cork out of the petrol tank, and fit a second cork with a slit cut in it as an air vent, pull the throttle valve (if the car is fitted with one) open to the fullest extent, put the switch into position and throw the motor out of gear . . .

To forget any one of these points will result in the car not starting, or stopping after a brief interval, and our readers would be surprised to learn how often this occurs through non-observance of these little points . . .

Then get your mixture as nearly right as you can guess at, and move the float up and down vigorously two or three times to pump a little vapour into the mixing chamber . . . to get this mixture absolutely correct, so as to give the best possible results, is exceedingly difficult. If the mixture errs on the rich side there may be explosions in the silencer . . .

In brief, the motorist should endeavour to get the best possible mixture, taking into consideration the speed required, and the gradient, and should always bear in mind that if he is in doubt on the subject it is best to err in the direction of too much air than of too much vapour.

. . . The car is now ready for starting, and only needs an impulse to give it motion. The two switches have closed up the gaps in the electric current, but for a spark to be produced in the plug the contact breaker has to act, and the piston has to draw in a charge of explosive mixture.

These operations are accomplished thus:-

(7) Put sparking advance in middle position. (8) Turn starting handle. (9) Manipulate sparking advance, so as to get the engine running at medium pace. (10)Throw on low gear.

(from de Dion owner's manual)

John Hissey sent me this photo (above) of his grandfather in his car with his son. David Burgess-Wise thought the car was an MMC circa 1902 and this was later confirmed by Mike Timms who owns "F 89", the sole surviving 1902 MMC 10hp pictured opposite. The date of the photo is of interest to John because the boy who looks about nine could either be his father who was born in 1898 or one of his uncles who were born in 1892 and 1896. It would have to be between 1902 and 1904 when registrations became compulsory.

MOON

Douglas Lowndes sent me this, thought to be an American Moon owned by his father in the mid 1920s. These were six cylinder cars with concealed door hinges and a radiator shape a bit like that of a Rolls Royce, all of which seem to fit. By 1924 they had Lockheed hydraulic brakes. And by 1925 a four bearing crankshaft, allowing an advertising boast: "You can hold your speedometer at 50–60 mph – or better if you dare – without vibration."

MORGAN

John Moore of Totnes sent in this photo of his father taken around 1920. The car was positively identified by Morgan enthusiast Jeremy Jones as a circa 1920 Morgan Grand Prix No 2 model fitted with a Swiss M.A.G. engine featuring overhead inlet and side exhaust valves. The Grand Prix was developed from the car in which W. G. McMinnies won the 1913 Cyclecar Grand Prix in Amiens, only to be later disqualified for entering a car the officials classified as a motorcycle and sidecar, not a cyclecar.

Roger Shapland of Henley-on-Thames sent this interesting photograph of a hill-climb (left), thought to have been taken in 1924. The car is being driven by Jack Hewens, a Maidenhead Morris dealer, with Stanley Shapland as "ballast". The question was, could the car be a one-off Cowley 11.9hp based Morris Special built by Hewens garage? Or was it one of the batch of six Cowley 11.9hp based MG Super Sports Morrises with bodies by Raworth of Oxford which were commissioned by Cecil Kimber in 1923? These were widely

advertised for their hill-climbing ability. David Potter, former chairman of the Vintage Register of the MG Car Club, identified the car as a Morris Sports Cowley of which 107 were built at a list price of £398-10s from 1921 to 1923. The extra wheels on the back are to aid traction. Harry Edwards, Historian of The Morris Register, sent me the above catalogue picture of the exact 1923 model with wing-top headlights, then retailing for 335 guineas and also the photo of a survivor "SV 7159" at a club event.

MOTORETTE

Charles Cadogan sought identification of this first-decade three-wheeler which his Swedish great grandfather purchased in Sweden in 1911 for SKR 2,100 (about £150). Identification came from Nick Georgano as a Motorette built by the C. W. Kelsey Manufacturing Co of Hartford Connecticut between 1910 and 1914. It had a 7hp air-cooled two cylinder engine with final drive by chain to the single rear wheel. About 210 were made.

PANHARD

Stephen Searle of Windsor sent this photo of a staged repair job. I thought it was a Belgian-built Germain 12hp of around 1903. But Stoke-on-Trent City Archives came up with the information that it was a 12hp Panhard, first registered to David Thomas in Stoke on Trent in 1906. It was then sold to Alfred McKay who converted it into a pick-up with signwriting "A.E. McKay – Windowblind Maker". The registration was cancelled in 1912.

PHOENIX

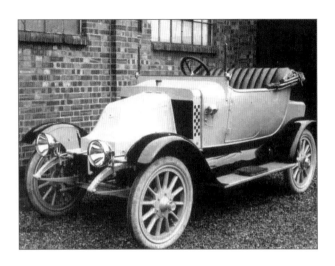 

All three pictures were taken in the Phoenix works during the 1920s. The picture on the left clearly shows a Phoenix 11.9hp, circa 1920, before it acquired a front mounted radiator. The other two pictures show a Phoenix 12/25, the company's last model built in any quantity. It had a 1,725cc Meadows four cylinder engine, glass sliding side windows and was built from 1922–24, with a few further examples after the company went into liquidation in 1924.

POPE TRIBUNE

L. Smerdon of Par in Cornwall sent me a very interesting and rare photograph of his late wife's grandparents, Jabez and Louisa Petherick, with their six children in an American Pope Tribune car. The Pethericks lived in Tavistock, Devon. Apparently Jabez went to the USA to purchase agricultural machinery and saw the Pope Tribune at the 1904 Automobile Exhibition in St. Louis. He then bought the sole rights to sell it in the UK, but before many had been sold the firm ceased production. The *Beaulieu Encyclopedia of the Automobile* says that the cars were built by Pope Manufacturing Co. of Hagerstown, Maryland between 1904 and 1908. Its first model was a runabout with a 6hp single cylinder engine, while the 1905 model was a 12hp two cylinder model with a 4 seater tonneau body.

RANGER

Identified as a Ranger – the Ranger was the West cyclecar of 1912 re-named. 1913 models were offered with air- or water-cooled two cylinder 964cc Precision engines with both bore and stroke of 85mm and a two speed gearbox with chain drive to the back axle. 1914 models had Blumfield twins or Alpha 4 engines. They were built by the Ranger Cyclecar Co. Ltd of Coventry from 1913 to 1914.

Paul Hambling of the Museum of Dartmoor Life asked about the car in this photo outside the garages of Day & Sons in Okehampton. "Y 155" is identified by David Burgess-Wise as probably a Regal, circa 1904.

RENAULT

The cars in this carefully composed photo were identified as a Renault (foreground),
a Daimler, a Sunbeam and another Daimler.

RILEY

Robert Leigh confirms this is a Riley 11hp. The Riley 10.8hp, 11hp or 11/40 was
built with successive name changes from 1919 to 1925 when it grew to the 11.9. It
had a 1,498cc side-valve four cylinder engine with detachable cylinder head and
four speed box. It was designed by Harry Rush and, in Nick Baldwin's words,
"was attractive and beautifully made". It formed the basis of the "Redwing" sports
car which was guaranteed to do 70mph.

ROLLS ROYCE

Richard Hewitt of Merryoaks, Co. Durham asked about this Rolls Royce owned by his father, Hinscliffe Hewitt, from 1945 to 1948. Bernard King of Complete Classics came back with the information that "GF5500" is an early 20/25 chassis delivered to Major J. Coats in 1930. Originally with Carlton Weymann saloon body, it received this 4-door cabriolet body by Compton in 1938. Wearing the later reg "SV5806", the car was recorded in Yucaipa, California in 1997.

Taken in Edinburgh in 1917 the photograph opposite shows a Rover 12hp drop-head coupé of around 1913 fitted with blackout lights in an attempt to thwart Zeppelin raids on the Leith and Rosyth dockyards. Many thanks to Mrs. S. Ives of Nicosia.

The car in the next picture (above left) was identified as a Rover Twelve tourer of 1919–1923. A 2,297cc four cylinder side valve engine made it reliable, but slow.

M. J. of London sought the identity of the car registered "DE 109" (above right), with her mother and grandmother aboard. It's a Rover 6hp of 1906-07, identified by the shape of its radiator cowl and its unusual steering column gearchange.

ROVER

Innes Sloss asked about this car with a "VA" registration (left), the photograph of which was taken in the 1920s or 1930s. It is a flat twin Rover 8HP.

Andrew Hodge of Blairgowrie sent the other picture (right) of a car owned by his late grandfather, Revd William Maxwell who was a Minister at Montrose in Angus, Scotland. It is a Rover 9/20hp, successor to the famous (infamous) Rover Eight but with a 1,075cc four cylinder engine rather than a flat twin.

SHEFFIELD SIMPLEX

John Wall of Palmerston in New Zealand asked about a car in which his grandfather, Henry Garner, was photographed. Of special interest is the front offside tyre, as Henry Garner claimed to have invented the first metal studded "non-skid" tyre for winter use. Having demonstrated its effectiveness on a London taxi driven over cobbled streets, he apparently sold the patent to Dunlop for £25,000, which he used to set up a factory in Birmingham to build Garner lorries. I am almost certain that the car depicted is a Sheffield Simplex 30hp of 1913.

SHEFFIELD SIMPLEX

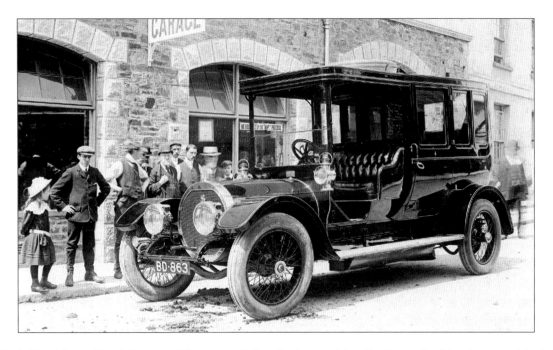

Paul Hambling of the Museum of Dartmoor Life asked me to identify the car in this photo outside the garages of Day & Sons in Okehampton. According to Henk Schuuring "BD 863" is an English Sheffield Simplex, confirmed by the double "S" on the radiator grille.

SIDDELEY DEASY

Identified as a Siddeley Deasy 18/24 or 24/3. The acetylene lights date it as pre-WW1. J. Siddeley joined the Deasy company in 1911 and the cars were known as Siddeley Deasys until 1919 when the company merged with Armstrong Whitworth of Newcastle-upon-Tyne and became Armstrong Siddeley.

SINGER

Identified as a 1908 Singer 7hp by Rudi de Groot of Gauteng, South Africa from a picture sent by Noel Thomas of St. Austell. The car had 2 cylinders 80 x 90mm, cone clutch, drive by prop shaft and differential. It was capable of 6mph in 1st; 12mph in 2nd; 24mph in 3rd.

John Carter's father owned this car while a rubber planter in Malaya in the early 1920s. It looks like a Singer 10/26hp, in production between 1925 and 1927 and a very popular model of which 15,500 were built. Only 1925 10/26 models lacked front brakes, so that pinpoints the year.

SORIANO-PEDROSO

Geoffrey Dellar sent me this photo of a rare Soriano-Pedroso taking part in the 42nd International Vintage and Veteran Car Rally at Barcelona in March 2000. These cars were built in France between 1919 and 1924 with 1,131cc or 1,590cc engines, though the 1,131 could be sleeved to under 1,100cc for Voiturette racing. The cars were unusual in retaining separate chain drives to each of the rear wheels.

THE DELICATE ESSENTIALS

Indispensable to the motorist who is going to drive her own car, is the overall. This should be made of butcher-blue or brown linen, to fasten at the back – the same shape as an artist's overall…

While there are several little repairs, that it would be impossible to remedy if wearing gloves, the majority of work on a car (filling tanks, etc., etc.) can be done just as well if one's hands are protected by a pair of wash-leather gloves. You will find room for these gloves in the little drawer under the seat of the car.

This little drawer is the secret of the dainty motorist. What you put in it depends on your tastes, but the following articles are what I advise you to have in its recesses. A pair of clean gloves, an extra handkerchief, clean veil, powder puff (unless you despise them), hair pins and ordinary pins, a hand-mirror – and some chocolates are very soothing, sometimes…

The mirror should be fairly large to be really useful, and it is better to have one with a handle to it … You will find it useful to have it handy – not for strictly personal use, but to occasionally hold it up to see what is behind you. Sometimes you will wonder if you heard a car behind you – and while the necessity or inclination to look round is rare, you can, with the mirror, see in a flash what is in the rear without losing your forward way, and without releasing your right-hand grip of the steering-wheel.

If you are going to drive alone in the highways and byways it might be advisable to carry a small revolver. I have an automatic 'Colt', and find it very easy to handle as there is practically no recoil – a great consideration to a woman. While I have never had occasion to use it on the road (though, I may add, I practice continually to keep my eye and hand 'in') it is nevertheless a comfort to know that should the occasion arise I have the means of defending myself.

(from The Woman and the Car, *by Dorothy Levitt, 1909)*

SPIJKER (SPYKER)

P. J. of Turrif, Aberdeenshire sent this photo of a Spyker, registered "0-2876". The car is a Spyker 14/18hp of around 1907, built by Jacobus Spyker at Trompenburg.

SPIJKER (SPYKER)

Pictured at Garage van Asselt in Amsterdam, "G-2500" was identified by Henk Schuuring as a 1910/1911 Spijker; the car in the background is a Renault.

The car on the left was confirmed by Leonard Barr of *The Standard Register* to be a 1914–19 Standard Model S 9.5hp with a 1,087cc four cylinder engine, bore and stroke 62 x 90. 1,936 were built and sold between 1913 and 1915. Production resumed in 1919, after which the stroke was increased to 110 raising the swept capacity to 1,328c and the model was re-named the "SLS" ("LS" for longer stroke).

The other car (right) was positively identified by Leonard Barr as a rare 8hp VI model of 1922. The engine had overhead valves and exposed pushrods which needed to be lubricated by hand every 200 miles. Only 500 were made and there are no survivors.

J. F. W. Bentley of Henley-in-Arden sent this photograph of his father in a bull-nosed car in which his mother used to take girl guides from Manchester to Llandudno. I'm almost certain the car is a Star, circa 1914 and probably a 15.9hp which had a 3,012cc side-valve four cylinder engine. But I could be wrong about the 15.9hp as Star was very prolific at the time and produced a plethora of different models.

This shows the grandfather of H. Corrall of Kingston-upon-Thames in a car from around the turn of the century. The driver was born in 1871 and the photograph was taken in Nottingham. Elizabeth Lawson of Edinburgh came to the rescue and identified the car as a Little Star of around 1905, made by the Star Engineering Company, Wolverhampton.

Anthony Judge of T. G. Beignton Ltd asked for identification of the car in the photograph with the two nurses, boyfriends and chaperones. The photo was taken at the Lodge Moor Isolation Hospital in Sheffield, which during WWI was turned into a Military Hospital. Henk Schuuring identified the car as a Straker-Squire 15hp or possibly the larger 20/25hp, circa 1918.

SWIFT

Ivor Bullock sent this photo of an earlier Mr Bullock in his car. "T94" was positively identified from Devon County Council records as first being used on a 9hp Clement tonneau with a green body, red wheels and registration to Frank Benyon. "T94" was later used from 1910 on a 7hp Swift 2-seater phaeton registered to Samuel Charles Bullock. He sold it to George Oram Webb who registered it for trade purposes in 1913. I guess that Sam Bullock bought the Clement and did not register it, then switched the plate to the Swift.

TALBOT

J. Gunn of Port St Mary, Isle of Man, sought the identity of this car, which I think is a
Talbot 15/20 or 25/50 built from 1913 until 1922.

This photo of a charabanc taken by professional photographer H. Greville of Maidenhead during the late 1920s/early1930s was sent in by Andy Steele. Tim Harding identified it as a Unic, circa 1922.

The car on the left is thought by Rupert Banner of Christie's to be a circa 1903 Vauxhall 5hp – one of the very first – of which around 40 were built. The price was 130 guineas, but for a further six guineas you could have a front seat as on the car shown. The engine was a horizontal single cylinder of 987cc, and springing was by coils.

The other car (right) was identified as a Vauxhall Light Six DY Twelve of 1935–36. It had a 1,530cc ohv six cylinder engine and a top speed of around 65mph.

Peter Parr of Lincoln sent this print of his father's car thought to be a Victor. The photo was taken just after WWI. It's an exact match for a Victor in the *Beaulieu Encyclopedia of the Automobile*. The Victor was originally called the Dew and was built by Victor Motors Ltd, Eynesford, Kent, from 1914 to 1915, then by Tyler Apparatus (Victor Motor Department) of Ealing, London. The original engine was a 965cc Precision V Twin, replaced in 1915 by an 1,100cc four. Only around 24 cars were built after WWI, possibly from left-over parts, and there are no records of any after 1920.

VULCAN

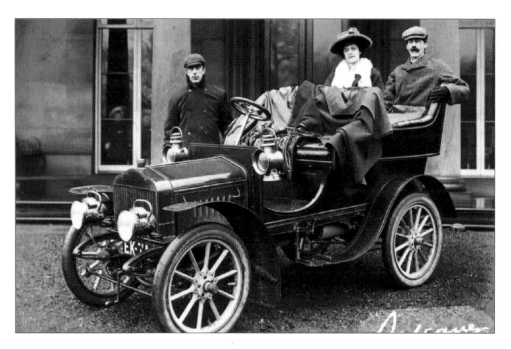

Peter Daniels initially identified this car as a Vulcan. It was then confirmed by Mike Worthington-Williams as a 12/14hp Vulcan tonneau.

Henk Schuuring identified this car as a Vulcan 14hp circa 1908/09.

WHITLOCK-ASTER

Mike Worthington-Williams and Malcolm Jeal identified this as a late 1905 or 1906 Whitlock-Aster, probably the 18/22 model, built in Holland Gate, London. This had a Whitlock body with a four cylinder Aster engine of 3,686cc and chain drive to the rear axle. A smaller 1,843cc 12/14 Whitlock-Aster finished 22nd in the 1905 Tourist Trophy.

ON PNEUMATIC TYRES

As we made our way out of London, over roads which were, on solid tyres, rough and uneven, I was bound to admit that pneumatic tyres were an improvement. We went along very gaily, and nothing happened.

Our spirits began to rise, and I had almost come to the conclusion that the experiment was an undoubted success, when with a loud report, one of the tyres collapsed . . . After wrestling with the outer cover for a long time, we eventually dismounted it, and found that, owing to the inner tube being very thin, a number of minute holes had been pinched in it through blowing down under pressure between the packing and the rim itself. We therefore had to patch the tube all the way round with long, thin strips of rubber. Then, to our horror, we notic-ed that the heat of the sun had apparently affected another tyre, and with a gasp it flattened out, even before we had finished the first one. Starting on the second, we found exactly the same trouble; and before we had repaired the second, we discovered that our first repair had been badly executed and that the tyre was again flat.

Our condition by this time was pitiable. We had been toiling for hours under a burning sun, without food and without the possibility of help from anywhere; and as a further catastrophe, a third tyre gave out. The pumping alone of these tyres required a vast amount of energy, especially as the back wheels were forty inches in diameter …We stuck to our task in the hope that eventually we should triumph over our troubles and be able to resume our journey, but a compact seemed to have been entered into between those tyres that on no account would they all stand up together. If we had two rights, No. 3 was wrong. When at last, we had the three tyres right, and had proceeded on our journey for about half a mile, No.4 gave up the ghost, and before No.4 was finished we found that No. 2 had again collapsed.

(from Ten Years of Motors and Motor Racing, *by Charles Jarrot, 1906)*

WOLSELEY

The photo on the left clearly features a Wolseley, thought to be a 24/30 of 1914 or 1915. Raymond Whittle of Northallerton identified the body as a Harrison All Weather type. R. Harrison & Son was established in 1883 in London NW1 and lasted until 1931. The company designed and built a range of standard bodies which it offered to various car makers.

The car on the right is thought to be either a Wolseley 7hp 1920–25 or a Wolseley 10hp 1922–25.

David Evans of Sevenoaks sent this photo of a car owned by his father, Captain C. G. Evans. It is a circa 1904 Wolseley designed by Herbert Austin and probaby a 10hp twin cylinder model of 2,593cc.

George Stanton of Aylesbury asked about this cyclecar which appears to be powered by a V-twin side-valve engine. Mike Worthington-Williams identified it as the prototype Worthington Runabout of 1909 to 1912, first powered by a 8hp flat twin and later by the transversely mounted 8/9hp JAP V-twin shown in the photo. It was planned to sell the car for £90, but it never went into production.

MYSTERIES AWAITING IDENTIFICATION

An identification for this car was sought by Peter Daniels. On the back of the print is inscribed "Mr and Mrs Bertram Bray (née Fanny Neale) and Miss Sarah Neale (sister)". Mike Worthington-Williams wonders if it is a Rexette, circa 1903–4.

V. Ibbett of St. Neots sent two old photographs. He thinks they were both taken around 1915. The first (above) shows a touring car, certainly American, with the same unusual rear canted bonnet louvres as seen on the Comet Six and 1918–19 Hupmobile. The second (opposite) shows a works pick-up truck, thought to have been bodied by Ibbetts on a Panhard-Levassor chassis.

This unidentified car was owned by the grandfather of Giles Pinnock.

Motor trader Jeff Way asked if the car in the picture could be the first Rambler. His relative, Thomas B. Jeffrey, left Plymouth in Devon to seek his fortune in the USA. Once there, with the help of R. Philip Gormully, he started building Rambler bicycles in Chicago. In 1897 Thomas Jeffrey and his son Charles Jeffrey built a light car powered by a single cylinder rear-mounted engine. This was followed in 1898 by a more advanced prototype with a two cylinder front-mounted engine.

Nigel Skellern sent me these photographs (above and opposite) of bodies built by F. Hearn & Co. (Bodybuilders) of Walsall where his grandfather, Stephen Skellern, worked from about 1903. The alloy bodied car in particular remains to be identified.

Max Jervis of Cheltenham asked about this car, apparently run by members of his family in North Staffordshire shortly after WWI.

Ann Stuart wanted to find out more about a motorhome commissioned by one of her ancestors, Albert Flekker of Ashton-under-Lyme. Apparently he had this one built on a Daimler chassis in 1913 at a total cost of £1,000. He specified the interior and left the exterior design to the coachbuilder. He wrote letters of complaint to Daimler in 1917 and 1919 because the wheels had cracked.

Roger Taylor sent this interesting picture of a Sunday family outing from Rochdale to Heaton Park, Manchester in 1902. It involved a round trip of about 10 miles during which anything less than two or three punctures was considered a fantastic success. I have been unable to identify the cars. At least 50 different makes and models had coalscuttle bonnets around this time but I can't find one with the same sharp edge to the front of the bonnet, no louvres on the front and long louvres at the sides.

Tim Salisbury of Deal, Kent sent me the photo on the left, taken circa 1910 of his great grandfather Charles Moykopf's car photographed outside the family home at Broadstairs. Henk Schuuring wonders if it is a Darracq 14-16HP of 1908– 1910/11. The extremely narrow rear door was unique to Darracq at the time.

Dennis Rigby-Bates sent the print (above right) of a car owned by cotton mill owner Joe Rivett of Stockport. His father was Rivett's chauffeur and mechanic in the 1920s and looked after three cars. One was a Calthorpe with a dickey seat, another was a Crossley 20hp two door sports saloon. The third was the car in the photograph which was apparently not a Rolls Royce 20hp despite looking very much like one.

Robert Hitchman of Freshwater, Isle of White found this photo among his late father's archives. Note the ABS (antiquated braking system). Obviously much of the contraption was home-built, but for identification purposes, I'll call it the pushmepullyou car.

D. Simpson of Whyteleafe sent a photograph (left) which he thinks depicts an Argyll owned by his grandfather in Scotland prior to WWI. It may well be, but I don't have an exact match.

Unfortunately the letter accompanying the photograph of Somerset registered "Y 53" (right) became separated and lost so I don't know who sent it.

Historian Wilf Aldridge sent the picture (left) of a very interesting mini-jeep photographed alongside the standard item during the Allied occupation of Japan soon after WWII. I think it is Japanese built and based on the license built Austin 7 Ruby based Datsun. Paul Seabury suggests that it could have been a Willys Jeep modified and built under licence by Mitsubishi, and therefore an ancestor of the Shogun in much the same way that the Range Rover of today grew out of a modified post-war copy of the wartime Willys and Ford Jeeps. Alternatively, Mike Worthington-Williams suggests that it could be an early Toyota Jeep, which, of course, grew into the Land Cruiser we know today.

The car in the other picture (right) was photographed outside "The American Steam Laundry" and is thought to be a pre WW1 Opel.

TEXTUAL SOURCES

Every effort has been made to contact all persons having any rights in the passages quoted in this book and to secure permission from the holders of such rights.

Quotation on page 22 ('An Apparition'), by A. B. Filson Young. First published in *The Complete Motorist*, Methuen & Co., 1904. Reprinted by permission of The Random House Group Ltd.

Quotation on page 41 ('Seating Arrangements'), by Kenneth Murchison. First published in *The Dawn of Motoring*, John Murray, 1942.

Quotation on page 65 ('The Gentle Art of Starting'), from de Dion owner's manual. Published in *The Dawn of Motoring*, John Murray, 1942.

Quotation on page 90 ('The Delicate Essentials'), by Dorothy Levitt. First published in *The Woman and the Car*, John Lane the Bodley Head, 1909.

Quotation on page 105 ('On Pneumatic Tyres'), by Charles Jarrot. First published in *Ten Years of Motors and Motor Racing*, Grant Richards, 1906.